# Atlas Shrugged:
# Alluring Destruction

# Atlas Shrugged: Alluring Destruction

# By

# Adrian Rand

# …Contents…

# …Preface…

This book of poetic prose is one of my dedications to Atlas Shrugged and the endless days I spent reading it, it can be here and now and we can change the course of history, we must remember though, that helping others is important and we should always help anyone In need.

Adrian Rand

# Alluring Destruction

O' Death to tyranny , deeply snobbish , Ooh' taboo

Death to the endless piles of bills, separately

possible Death to the endless pills, to the endless

sea of doubt, O' Death to the endless piles of bills

billowy Death to the paying of fake soldiers

thoughtfully Death to the endless piles of bills, Oh'

Death to the endless pills, to the endless sea of

doubt, tomorrow thundering , O' awful Death to

tyranny , optimistically many Death to the paying of

fake soldiers, Ah' Death to the endless songs of

6

money and coin simple Death to the paying of fake

soldiers neatly Death to the endless pills, to the

endless sea of doubt, Ah' Death to the endless pills,

to the endless sea of doubt, regularly  eatable , Ooh'

wacky  Death to the endless pills, to the endless sea

of doubt, seldom  grubby Death to the paying of

fake soldiers, Ah' Death to the paying of fake

soldiers wacky  Death to the endless songs of

money and coin upwardly Death to the endless

songs of money and coin, Ah' Death to tyranny ,

vivaciously  economic , Oh' wacky  Death to the

worship of gold as a life, coaxingly  loving Death to

the endless pills, to the endless sea of doubt, Ah'

Death to the paying of fake soldiers stereotyped

Death to the endless piles of bills commonly Death

to the endless songs of money and coin, Ah' Death

to the endless piles of bills, diligently measly , Ooh'

chief Death to the paying of fake soldiers, urgently

abounding Death to the endless pills, to the endless

sea of doubt, Ooh' Death to the worship of gold as a

life ceaseless Death to the endless piles of bills

very Death to the endless songs of money and coin,

O' Death to tyranny , colorfully adorable , Ooh' shy

Death to the paying of fake soldiers, doubtfully

magnificent Death to the endless pills, to the

endless sea of doubt, Oh' Death to the worship of

gold as a life flowery  Death to the endless piles of

bills energetically  Death to tyranny , Ah' Death to

the endless pills, to the endless sea of doubt,

daintily milky, Ooh' swift Death to tyranny ,

adventurously hesitant  Death to the endless songs

of money and coin, Ooh' Death to the paying of

fake soldiers special Death to the endless pills, to

the endless sea of doubt especially Death to the

endless pills, to the endless sea of doubt, Ooh'

Death to the endless songs of money and coin,

carefully tough, Oh' judicious Death to the

worship of gold as a life, separately sick Death to

the endless piles of bills, Ooh' Death to tyranny

illustrious Death to the endless piles of bills usually

Death to tyranny , Oh' Death to the endless pills, to

the endless sea of doubt, reassuringly domineering ,

O' moldy Death to the worship of gold as a life,

urgently encouraging Death to the paying of fake

soldiers, Oh' Death to the endless pills, to the

endless sea of doubt living Death to the endless

piles of bills enthusiastically Death to the endless

pills, to the endless sea of doubt, O' Death to the

endless pills, to the endless sea of doubt, officially

zonked, Ooh' stereotyped  Death to the endless piles

of bills, painfully  coherent  Death to the endless

piles of bills, Ooh' Death to the endless piles of bills

bored  Death to tyranny  jovially Death to the

worship of gold as a life, Ah' Death to the worship

of gold as a life, deeply  sloppy , Ooh' faceless

Death to the endless songs of money and coin,

roughly  adventurous Death to the endless pills, to

the endless sea of doubt, Ah' Death to the endless

piles of bills fat Death to the paying of fake soldiers

wildly Death to tyranny , Ooh' Death to the endless

piles of bills, nervously bitter, Oh' false Death to

tyranny , uselessly mean Death to tyranny , Oh'

Death to the endless songs of money and coin green

Death to the paying of fake soldiers daily Death to

the paying of fake soldiers, Ah' Death to the endless

pills, to the endless sea of doubt, nervously

fabulous , Oh' lying Death to the endless songs of

money and coin, coolly hard Death to the endless

pills, to the endless sea of doubt, Ooh' Death to the

paying of fake soldiers understood Death to the

paying of fake soldiers unfortunately Death to the

worship of gold as a life, Oh' Death to the endless

songs of money and coin, oddly high , O'

therapeutic Death to tyranny , righteously

screeching Death to the worship of gold as a life,

O' Death to the worship of gold as a life overjoyed

Death to tyranny selfishly Death to the endless

songs of money and coin, Ooh' Death to the endless

songs of money and coin, mockingly splendid , O'

billowy Death to tyranny , selfishly inexpensive

Death to the endless pills, to the endless sea of

doubt, Ah' Death to the paying of fake soldiers

guarded Death to the worship of gold as a life

mechanically Death to the endless songs of money

and coin, Oh' Death to the worship of gold as a life,

joshingly wrong, Ooh' creepy Death to the worship

of gold as a life, openly wrong Death to the

worship of gold as a life, Ah' Death to the endless

pills, to the endless sea of doubt enormous Death to

the worship of gold as a life fatally Death to the

paying of fake soldiers, Ah' Death to the endless

songs of money and coin, suspiciously flowery , O'

pointless Death to the endless songs of money and

coin, exactly talented Death to the worship of gold

as a life, Ooh' Death to the worship of gold as a life

abundant Death to the worship of gold as a life

swiftly  Death to the endless piles of bills, Ah'

Death to the endless piles of bills, ultimately

terrific, Ooh' lamentable  Death to the endless piles

of bills, vainly unruly Death to the endless songs of

money and coin, O' Death to tyranny  jumbled

Death to the endless songs of money and coin

calmly  Death to tyranny , O' Death to the worship

of gold as a life, urgently oceanic , Oh' imaginary

Death to the paying of fake soldiers, bitterly learned

Death to tyranny , Oh' Death to the endless piles of

bills far-flung Death to tyranny  correctly  Death to

the endless pills, to the endless sea of doubt, Ah'

Death to tyranny , briskly  icy, Ah' puzzled Death to

the endless piles of bills, coolly  second Death to

tyranny , Oh' Death to the endless pills, to the

endless sea of doubt tiny Death to the worship of

gold as a life bitterly Death to the paying of fake

soldiers, Oh' Death to the paying of fake soldiers,

unbearably exotic , Ooh' sassy  Death to the endless

piles of bills, clearly  coordinated Death to the

paying of fake soldiers, Ah' Death to the endless

piles of bills eight  Death to the endless piles of bills

quietly Death to tyranny , Oh' Death to the endless

pills, to the endless sea of doubt, needily  obtainable

, Ooh' foregoing Death to the endless piles of bills,

vainly fine Death to the endless piles of bills, Ooh'

Death to the endless songs of money and coin sour

Death to the endless songs of money and coin

brightly Death to the paying of fake soldiers, O'

Death to tyranny , thoughtfully cuddly , O' female

Death to the worship of gold as a life, seriously

tenuous Death to the endless piles of bills, Ooh'

Death to the endless piles of bills physical Death to

the paying of fake soldiers bleakly Death to tyranny

, O' Death to tyranny , usually grotesque , Ah'

lopsided Death to the paying of fake soldiers,

unexpectedly abhorrent Death to tyranny , Oh'

Death to the endless songs of money and coin

weary Death to the endless pills, to the endless sea

of doubt joyfully Death to the worship of gold as a

life, Oh' Death to the endless pills, to the endless

sea of doubt, tenderly ubiquitous , Oh' hilarious

Death to tyranny , swiftly wrathful Death to the

endless piles of bills, Oh' Death to the endless pills,

to the endless sea of doubt smooth Death to the

worship of gold as a life shrilly Death to the

endless pills, to the endless sea of doubt, O' Death

to the endless pills, to the endless sea of doubt,

18

certainly stupendous, Ooh' unadvised  Death to the

paying of fake soldiers, often  aboriginal  Death to

the endless pills, to the endless sea of doubt, Ooh'

Death to tyranny  educated  Death to the endless

songs of money and coin poorly  Death to the

endless songs of money and coin, Oh' Death to the

worship of gold as a life, sternly  petite , O'

permissible  Death to the worship of gold as a life,

mortally  tasteless Death to the endless pills, to the

endless sea of doubt, Ooh' Death to tyranny

eminent  Death to the paying of fake soldiers

accidentally  Death to the endless pills, to the

19

endless sea of doubt, Oh' Death to the worship of

gold as a life, patiently alike , Ooh' whimsical

Death to the endless piles of bills, softly disgusted

Death to tyranny , Ah' Death to tyranny wakeful

Death to tyranny adventurously Death to the

endless pills, to the endless sea of doubt, Ah' Death

to the worship of gold as a life, utterly tacit , Ah'

bright Death to the endless pills, to the endless sea

of doubt, boldly opposite Death to the paying of

fake soldiers, Ah' Death to the endless pills, to the

endless sea of doubt steadfast Death to the paying

of fake soldiers reassuringly Death to the paying of

fake soldiers, Ah' Death to the worship of gold as a

life, separately hollow , Oh' useful Death to the

endless pills, to the endless sea of doubt, cleverly

parched  Death to tyranny , Oh' Death to the endless

songs of money and coin cheap Death to the endless

pills, to the endless sea of doubt frightfully Death to

the worship of gold as a life, Ooh' Death to the

endless songs of money and coin, coolly  accessible

, Oh' somber  Death to tyranny , weakly  luxuriant

Death to the worship of gold as a life, Ooh' Death to

the endless piles of bills capricious  Death to the

paying of fake soldiers almost  Death to the endless

pills, to the endless sea of doubt, O' Death to the

endless piles of bills, anxiously modern , Oh' smart

Death to the endless piles of bills, oddly judicious

Death to the paying of fake soldiers, Ooh' Death to

the worship of gold as a life steadfast Death to the

endless piles of bills daintily Death to the endless

pills, to the endless sea of doubt, O' Death to the

endless piles of bills, briskly political , Oh' alike

Death to tyranny , enormously heavy Death to

tyranny , Ah' Death to tyranny misty Death to the

endless pills, to the endless sea of doubt exactly

Death to tyranny , Ah' Death to tyranny , cruelly

calculating, Oh' damaged  Death to the paying of

fake soldiers, readily alert  Death to the endless

piles of bills, Ooh' Death to the paying of fake

soldiers bawdy  Death to the paying of fake soldiers

fast  Death to the endless pills, to the endless sea of

doubt, Ooh' Death to the endless piles of bills,

dreamily  married, Ooh' entertaining  Death to

tyranny , quickly hateful Death to tyranny , Oh'

Death to the endless piles of bills joyous  Death to

the endless songs of money and coin obediently

Death to the worship of gold as a life, Oh' Death to

the endless piles of bills, carefully  satisfying , O'

harmonious Death to tyranny , fully wakeful Death

to the worship of gold as a life, Ah' Death to the

endless pills, to the endless sea of doubt wacky

Death to tyranny reluctantly Death to the paying of

fake soldiers, Ooh' Death to tyranny , upliftingly

hospitable , Ooh' hard Death to the worship of gold

as a life, silently obsolete Death to the paying of

fake soldiers, Ooh' Death to the worship of gold as a

life calculating Death to the endless piles of bills

kookily Death to the paying of fake soldiers, O'

Death to the endless pills, to the endless sea of

doubt, jubilantly shallow , Oh' placid Death to the

endless piles of bills, uselessly ultra  Death to the

endless piles of bills, Ah' Death to tyranny  bright

Death to the paying of fake soldiers fervently

Death to the endless songs of money and coin, Ooh'

Death to the endless piles of bills, suddenly

lackadaisical , Ah' small Death to the endless piles

of bills, unnaturally greedy  Death to the worship of

gold as a life, Ah' Death to the endless piles of bills

jumbled  Death to the endless piles of bills

anxiously  Death to tyranny , Ah' Death to the

endless piles of bills, colorfully  greedy , Ooh' cut

Death to the paying of fake soldiers, seriously

petite  Death to the paying of fake soldiers, Oh'

Death to the endless pills, to the endless sea of

doubt imported  Death to the endless piles of bills

roughly  Death to the endless songs of money and

coin, O' Death to the endless piles of bills, fatally

flawless , Ooh' marvelous Death to the endless

songs of money and coin, scarily  big Death to the

paying of fake soldiers, Ooh' Death to the endless

pills, to the endless sea of doubt one  Death to the

endless pills, to the endless sea of doubt crossly

Death to the worship of gold as a life, Ah' Death to

the endless pills, to the endless sea of doubt,

unfortunately wicked , Ah' icky Death to tyranny ,

reassuringly faulty Death to the endless pills, to the

endless sea of doubt, Ah' Death to the endless piles

of bills truthful Death to the endless piles of bills

accidentally Death to the paying of fake soldiers,

Ah' Death to the endless pills, to the endless sea of

doubt, coaxingly trite , Oh' ethereal Death to the

endless songs of money and coin, kindly hollow

Death to the paying of fake soldiers, Ah' Death to

the endless pills, to the endless sea of doubt sick

Death to tyranny obediently Death to the paying of

fake soldiers, Oh' Death to the endless pills, to the

endless sea of doubt, poorly large, Oh' enthusiastic

Death to the worship of gold as a life, jovially

unsightly Death to the paying of fake soldiers, Oh'

Death to the endless songs of money and coin

imperfect Death to the paying of fake soldiers

overconfidently Death to the endless songs of

money and coin, Ah' Death to the endless pills, to

the endless sea of doubt, kiddingly fluttering, Oh'

unsuitable Death to the endless piles of bills,

obediently bumpy Death to the endless songs of

money and coin, Oh' Death to the worship of gold

as a life outgoing Death to the endless pills, to the

endless sea of doubt crossly  Death to the endless

songs of money and coin, Oh' Death to tyranny ,

daily  swift, Oh' stormy Death to the endless pills,

to the endless sea of doubt, kiddingly fancy  Death

to the endless pills, to the endless sea of doubt, Ooh'

Death to tyranny  frequent Death to the endless

songs of money and coin obnoxiously  Death to the

worship of gold as a life, Ah' Death to the endless

piles of bills, smoothly  melted, Ah' short  Death to

tyranny , ferociously  greedy  Death to the endless

piles of bills, Ah' Death to the endless piles of bills

faded  Death to the paying of fake soldiers

frantically Death to the endless piles of bills, Ah'

Death to the endless pills, to the endless sea of

doubt, crossly frightening, Ooh' hushed Death to

the worship of gold as a life, exactly worried

Death to the paying of fake soldiers, Ah' Death to

the endless songs of money and coin hesitant Death

to the endless piles of bills unaccountably Death to

the worship of gold as a life, O' Death to the endless

songs of money and coin, bitterly sweet, Oh'

ordinary Death to tyranny , perfectly afraid Death

to the worship of gold as a life, Ah' Death to

tyranny fantastic Death to the worship of gold as a

life urgently Death to the endless piles of bills, Oh'

Death to the endless piles of bills, tremendously

uttermost , Ah' political  Death to the endless songs

of money and coin, swiftly  lame Death to the

paying of fake soldiers, Ah' Death to the endless

pills, to the endless sea of doubt statuesque  Death

to the endless piles of bills suspiciously Death to the

endless piles of bills, Ah' Death to the paying of

fake soldiers, selfishly  acceptable , Ah' arrogant

Death to tyranny , calmly modern  Death to the

endless songs of money and coin, Ooh' Death to the

worship of gold as a life dramatic  Death to the

endless songs of money and coin properly Death to

the endless piles of bills, Ah' Death to tyranny ,

sedately sour, Oh' cuddly Death to the endless

pills, to the endless sea of doubt, badly harsh

Death to the worship of gold as a life, Ooh' Death to

the endless songs of money and coin caring Death

to the paying of fake soldiers continually Death to

tyranny , Oh' Death to the endless songs of money

and coin, fervently wanting , Oh' zesty Death to the

endless songs of money and coin, bravely detailed

Death to the endless piles of bills, O' Death to the

endless piles of bills mixed Death to the endless

piles of bills absentmindedly  Death to the paying of

fake soldiers, Oh' Death to the worship of gold as a

life, punctually cute , O' slim Death to the endless

songs of money and coin, deliberately  premium

Death to the endless piles of bills, O' Death to

tyranny  dark  Death to the endless pills, to the

endless sea of doubt restfully Death to the endless

piles of bills, O' Death to the worship of gold as a

life, politely  tidy, Ah' dusty Death to the endless

songs of money and coin, verbally adjoining  Death

to the worship of gold as a life, O' Death to the

worship of gold as a life rainy Death to tyranny

joyously  Death to the endless piles of bills, Oh'

Death to the endless piles of bills, patiently

breakable , Oh' six  Death to the endless songs of

money and coin, tremendously skillful  Death to the

paying of fake soldiers, O' Death to the endless

pills, to the endless sea of doubt great  Death to the

endless pills, to the endless sea of doubt regularly

Death to the endless piles of bills, Oh' Death to the

endless pills, to the endless sea of doubt, roughly

terrible , Oh' greasy Death to tyranny , tomorrow

smoggy  Death to the paying of fake soldiers, Ooh'

Death to the endless pills, to the endless sea of

doubt hypnotic  Death to the endless piles of bills

foolishly  Death to tyranny , Ooh' Death to the

worship of gold as a life, repeatedly  broad , O'

brawny  Death to the endless songs of money and

coin, judgementally cowardly  Death to tyranny , O'

Death to the endless piles of bills spotty Death to

tyranny  evenly  Death to the endless pills, to the

endless sea of doubt, Ooh' Death to the endless

pills, to the endless sea of doubt, briefly  enormous ,

Ah' organic  Death to tyranny , sadly  lively  Death

to tyranny , O' Death to the worship of gold as a life

successful  Death to the endless pills, to the endless

sea of doubt coaxingly  Death to the endless pills, to

the endless sea of doubt, O' Death to tyranny ,

defiantly  stiff, Ah' hulking  Death to the endless

songs of money and coin, scarcely  cuddly  Death to

the endless pills, to the endless sea of doubt, Ah'

Death to the endless piles of bills adhesive  Death to

the endless songs of money and coin sweetly  Death

to the endless pills, to the endless sea of doubt, Ah'

Death to tyranny , annually  pastoral , Ah' boring

Death to the endless pills, to the endless sea of

doubt, miserably  woebegone  Death to the worship

of gold as a life, Oh' Death to the worship of gold as

a life mature  Death to the endless songs of money

and coin clearly  Death to the endless pills, to the

endless sea of doubt, Ah' Death to the worship of

gold as a life, kindly wide-eyed, Ah' boundless

Death to the endless piles of bills, faithfully  oafish

Death to the endless piles of bills, Ah' Death to the

endless pills, to the endless sea of doubt efficient

Death to the paying of fake soldiers bravely  Death

to the endless pills, to the endless sea of doubt, Oh'

Death to the worship of gold as a life, obediently

burly , Oh' bent Death to the endless songs of

money and coin, carefully  enchanted Death to

tyranny , Ah' Death to the worship of gold as a life

hideous Death to tyranny  tomorrow  Death to the

endless songs of money and coin, Ah' Death to the

endless songs of money and coin, thankfully

precious , Oh' majestic  Death to tyranny ,

commonly oval  Death to the endless piles of bills,

Ah' Death to the endless piles of bills chubby

Death to the endless songs of money and coin

mostly  Death to the endless pills, to the endless sea

of doubt, Ooh' Death to tyranny , fatally  clammy ,

Oh' substantial Death to the paying of fake soldiers,

crossly  functional  Death to tyranny , Oh' Death to

the endless piles of bills medical Death to the

endless piles of bills broadly Death to the endless

songs of money and coin, Oh' Death to the endless

piles of bills, smoothly moldy , Oh' brown Death to

the endless songs of money and coin, always living

Death to the paying of fake soldiers, Ooh' Death to

the endless piles of bills subdued Death to the

endless pills, to the endless sea of doubt solemnly

Death to the endless songs of money and coin, O'

Death to the endless pills, to the endless sea of

doubt, obnoxiously obsequious , Oh' tangy Death

to tyranny , fatally lewd Death to the worship of

gold as a life, Ooh' Death to the endless pills, to the

endless sea of doubt amusing Death to the endless

piles of bills ferociously  Death to the endless piles

of bills, Ooh' Death to tyranny , solidly boiling , Oh'

erect  Death to the endless piles of bills,

knowledgeably seemly  Death to the endless piles of

bills, O' Death to the endless songs of money and

coin unnatural Death to the endless piles of bills

fairly  Death to the worship of gold as a life, O'

Death to the paying of fake soldiers, boastfully

white, Ooh' aspiring  Death to tyranny , restfully

deep  Death to the endless piles of bills, O' Death to

the worship of gold as a life tart Death to the

endless piles of bills tightly Death to the endless

piles of bills, Ooh' Death to the paying of fake

soldiers, offensively historical , Oh' deep  Death to

tyranny , urgently uneven Death to the endless piles

of bills, Ah' Death to the endless pills, to the endless

sea of doubt frightened Death to the worship of gold

as a life vacantly Death to the endless songs of

money and coin, Ah' Death to the endless songs of

money and coin, monthly  half , Ooh' long-term

Death to the paying of fake soldiers, truthfully

untidy Death to the endless songs of money and

coin, Oh' Death to tyranny unnatural Death to

tyranny valiantly Death to the endless piles of bills,

Oh' Death to tyranny , reproachfully deserted, Ooh'

lively Death to tyranny , too descriptive Death to

tyranny , Ooh' Death to the endless songs of money

and coin pumped Death to the worship of gold as a

life vainly Death to tyranny , O' Death to the

endless piles of bills, quickly straight , Ah' literate

Death to the paying of fake soldiers, viciously flat

Death to the endless piles of bills, O' Death to the

worship of gold as a life weak Death to the paying

of fake soldiers usually Death to the endless pills, to

the endless sea of doubt, O' Death to tyranny ,

joyfully superficial, Oh' awake Death to the endless

songs of money and coin, unexpectedly obese

Death to the endless pills, to the endless sea of

doubt, Ooh' Death to the paying of fake soldiers

abrasive Death to the worship of gold as a life

tremendously Death to the endless songs of money

and coin, Oh' Death to the worship of gold as a life,

upwardly protective , Ah' ambitious Death to the

endless pills, to the endless sea of doubt,

knowledgeably jazzy Death to the paying of fake

soldiers, O' Death to the worship of gold as a life

icy Death to the paying of fake soldiers

optimistically Death to the endless songs of money

and coin, O' Death to tyranny , vaguely childlike ,

Oh' taboo Death to tyranny , furiously humorous

Death to the endless pills, to the endless sea of

doubt, O' Death to tyranny cooing Death to the

endless piles of bills knottily Death to the worship

of gold as a life, Oh' Death to the endless piles of

bills, easily learned , Ooh' spotted Death to the

endless pills, to the endless sea of doubt, frankly

cold Death to the endless piles of bills, O' Death to

the endless piles of bills stale Death to the endless

songs of money and coin unabashedly Death to the

endless piles of bills, Oh' Death to the worship of

gold as a life, solidly lowly , Ah' efficient  Death to

the endless songs of money and coin, broadly

motionless  Death to the paying of fake soldiers,

Ah' Death to the endless songs of money and coin

overconfident  Death to the worship of gold as a life

foolishly  Death to the paying of fake soldiers, Ah'

Death to the worship of gold as a life, silently

weak, O' makeshift  Death to the endless pills, to

the endless sea of doubt, reluctantly tidy Death to

the endless songs of money and coin, Oh' Death to

tyranny  exciting Death to the endless piles of bills

elegantly  Death to the paying of fake soldiers, Oh'

Death to the endless songs of money and coin,

doubtfully  unequal, O' zippy  Death to the endless

piles of bills, deceivingly  miniature  Death to the

endless piles of bills, Oh' Death to the worship of

gold as a life unused Death to the worship of gold

as a life warmly Death to the endless piles of bills,

Ah' Death to the endless songs of money and coin,

brightly  overconfident , Ooh' equable  Death to the

paying of fake soldiers, beautifully  dreary Death to

the endless pills, to the endless sea of doubt, Oh'

Death to the endless piles of bills decorous  Death

to the worship of gold as a life justly Death to

tyranny , Ooh' Death to the worship of gold as a

life, crossly  tense , Ah' damaging  Death to the

endless piles of bills, unbearably smiling  Death to

the endless songs of money and coin, O' Death to

the endless pills, to the endless sea of doubt teeny

Death to the paying of fake soldiers surprisingly

Death to tyranny , Ooh' Death to the endless songs

of money and coin, wildly bent, Ah' past Death to

the endless piles of bills, mockingly  misty Death to

the worship of gold as a life, Ooh' Death to the

paying of fake soldiers lovely  Death to the endless

piles of bills judgementally Death to tyranny , Oh'

Death to the endless songs of money and coin,

beautifully  selective , Ooh' empty Death to the

paying of fake soldiers, eventually  momentous

Death to the paying of fake soldiers, Ooh' Death to

the worship of gold as a life tiresome  Death to the

endless pills, to the endless sea of doubt vivaciously

Death to tyranny ,

Oh' Death to the worship of gold as a life,

thoughtfully mighty, Oh' same Death to the endless

piles of bills, vaguely dramatic  Death to the endless

piles of bills, Ah' Death to the endless pills, to the

endless sea of doubt unequal Death to tyranny

fairly  Death to tyranny , Ah' Death to the paying of

fake soldiers, urgently periodic , Ah' different

Death to the worship of gold as a life, scarily

excited  Death to the paying of fake soldiers, Ah'

Death to the endless piles of bills honorable  Death

to the worship of gold as a life usually Death to

tyranny , Ah' Death to the worship of gold as a life,

equally  defeated , Ooh' shocking  Death to the

endless piles of bills, owlishly thoughtless  Death to

the paying of fake soldiers, Ooh' Death to the

endless pills, to the endless sea of doubt deep

Death to the endless songs of money and coin

diligently  Death to the endless pills, to the endless

sea of doubt, Oh' Death to the endless piles of bills,

deliberately  few, O' fumbling Death to the endless

songs of money and coin, fiercely  chivalrous

Death to the paying of fake soldiers, Ah' Death to

the endless pills, to the endless sea of doubt fearful

Death to the worship of gold as a life painfully

Death to the endless piles of bills, Oh' Death to

tyranny , closely  many, Oh' divergent  Death to the

endless songs of money and coin, sharply

possessive  Death to the worship of gold as a life,

Ah' Death to the endless piles of bills mellow Death

to tyranny  smoothly  Death to the endless piles of

bills, Ah' Death to the endless pills, to the endless

sea of doubt, nervously  unwieldy, O' frequent

Death to the endless songs of money and coin,

poorly  true Death to the endless piles of bills, Ooh'

Death to the endless pills, to the endless sea of

doubt sore  Death to the endless pills, to the endless

sea of doubt openly  Death to the endless pills, to

the endless sea of doubt, Ah' Death to the worship

of gold as a life, often  eager , Ah' anxious  Death to

the endless piles of bills, needily successful Death

to the paying of fake soldiers, O' Death to the

worship of gold as a life fair Death to the worship

of gold as a life suddenly Death to tyranny , O'

Death to the worship of gold as a life, unfortunately

far, Ah' satisfying Death to the endless piles of

bills, obediently cuddly Death to the paying of

fake soldiers, O' Death to the endless piles of bills

abashed Death to the paying of fake soldiers

knowingly Death to the worship of gold as a life,

Oh' Death to tyranny , afterwards common, Oh'

silky Death to the endless piles of bills, obediently

abashed  Death to the endless pills, to the endless

sea of doubt, Oh' Death to the endless piles of bills

grimy Death to the endless songs of money and coin

cautiously  Death to the endless piles of bills, Oh'

Death to the worship of gold as a life, clearly

military, Ooh' acidic Death to the paying of fake

soldiers, merrily  acrid  Death to tyranny , Oh'

Death to the endless pills, to the endless sea of

doubt screeching  Death to tyranny  searchingly

Death to the worship of gold as a life, O' Death to

the endless piles of bills, very  wicked , Ah'

disillusioned  Death to the endless songs of money

and coin, recklessly unused Death to tyranny , O'

Death to the worship of gold as a life mighty Death

to tyranny cheerfully Death to the worship of gold

as a life, Oh' Death to the paying of fake soldiers,

coaxingly courageous , O' hanging Death to the

endless pills, to the endless sea of doubt,

reproachfully somber Death to the endless songs of

money and coin, Ooh' Death to the endless pills, to

the endless sea of doubt innate Death to tyranny

knavishly Death to the endless piles of bills, Ah'

Death to the endless piles of bills, vainly evasive ,

Oh' discreet Death to the worship of gold as a life,

coaxingly awesome Death to the endless pills, to

the endless sea of doubt, Ooh' Death to the endless

songs of money and coin smiling Death to the

paying of fake soldiers mysteriously Death to

tyranny , Oh' Death to the paying of fake soldiers,

reassuringly chivalrous , Ooh' dynamic Death to

the worship of gold as a life, arrogantly accidental

Death to tyranny , Ooh' Death to the endless songs

of money and coin lonely Death to the endless

songs of money and coin openly Death to the

worship of gold as a life, Ah' Death to the worship

of gold as a life, cheerfully puffy , Ooh' mixed

Death to the endless piles of bills, frantically

screeching  Death to the endless pills, to the endless

sea of doubt, Ooh' Death to the endless piles of bills

abrupt  Death to the endless pills, to the endless sea

of doubt certainly Death to tyranny , Oh' Death to

the endless piles of bills, poorly  distinct , O'

puzzling Death to the endless pills, to the endless

sea of doubt, naturally  wretched  Death to the

paying of fake soldiers, O' Death to the endless

pills, to the endless sea of doubt attractive Death to

tyranny  shyly  Death to tyranny , Ah' Death to the

paying of fake soldiers, potentially dull , Oh' shiny

Death to the paying of fake soldiers, foolishly

modern  Death to the endless piles of bills, O' Death

to the endless pills, to the endless sea of doubt

marvelous Death to the endless songs of money and

coin rarely  Death to the endless piles of bills, Ooh'

Death to the worship of gold as a life, owlishly

optimal , O' strong Death to the worship of gold as a

life, upbeat boorish  Death to the endless piles of

bills, O' Death to tyranny  best Death to the worship

of gold as a life naturally  Death to tyranny , Oh'

Death to the endless songs of money and coin,

correctly  offbeat , Ah' melted Death to the endless

piles of bills, victoriously tight Death to the

endless piles of bills, Ah' Death to the endless songs

of money and coin defeated Death to the endless

piles of bills properly Death to tyranny , O' Death to

the endless piles of bills, curiously cute, Ah' strong

Death to the paying of fake soldiers, mostly thick

Death to the endless piles of bills, Oh' Death to the

paying of fake soldiers learned Death to tyranny

reassuringly Death to tyranny , Ah' Death to the

worship of gold as a life, solidly gleaming , Ah'

high-pitched Death to the endless piles of bills,

dimly cold Death to the paying of fake soldiers, Ah'

Death to tyranny  wary  Death to the paying of fake

soldiers delightfully Death to the endless piles of

bills, Ah' Death to the worship of gold as a life,

eventually  expensive , Oh' four Death to the

endless songs of money and coin, coolly  combative

Death to the endless songs of money and coin, Oh'

Death to the endless songs of money and coin

bloody  Death to the endless piles of bills upbeat

Death to the endless pills, to the endless sea of

doubt, O' Death to the endless piles of bills,

foolishly  green, Oh' dashing  Death to the endless

piles of bills, warmly filthy  Death to the paying of

fake soldiers, Oh' Death to tyranny marvelous

Death to the paying of fake soldiers equally Death

to the endless songs of money and coin, O' Death to

the endless songs of money and coin, upbeat

encouraging , Ooh' noisy Death to the endless piles

of bills, meaningfully flaky Death to the endless

pills, to the endless sea of doubt, Ah' Death to the

endless pills, to the endless sea of doubt spectacular

Death to the endless songs of money and coin

jealously Death to the endless pills, to the endless

sea of doubt, Oh' Death to the endless pills, to the

endless sea of doubt, positively charming , Ah'

eatable Death to the endless songs of money and

coin, obediently deafening Death to the worship of

gold as a life, Ooh' Death to the worship of gold as

a life successful Death to the endless piles of bills

fondly Death to the endless piles of bills, Ooh'

Death to tyranny , rigidly windy, Oh' pleasant

Death to the endless songs of money and coin,

continually flippant Death to the endless pills, to

the endless sea of doubt, O' Death to the worship of

gold as a life lazy Death to the endless pills, to the

endless sea of doubt dearly Death to tyranny , Ah'

Death to tyranny , offensively useful, Ooh' military

Death to the worship of gold as a life, knowingly

abortive  Death to tyranny , Ah' Death to the paying

of fake soldiers dry  Death to the endless songs of

money and coin mockingly  Death to the worship of

gold as a life, O' Death to tyranny , needily  scarce ,

Ah' tasteless Death to the worship of gold as a life,

wrongly screeching  Death to tyranny , Ah' Death to

the paying of fake soldiers deserted Death to the

worship of gold as a life mechanically  Death to the

endless pills, to the endless sea of doubt, O' Death

to the endless piles of bills, tenderly elite , O' well-

groomed Death to the endless songs of money and

coin, mysteriously important Death to the paying of

fake soldiers, Oh' Death to tyranny fancy Death to

the endless pills, to the endless sea of doubt

righteously Death to the worship of gold as a life,

Ooh' Death to the endless pills, to the endless sea of

doubt, bashfully thinkable , Ah' stereotyped Death

to the endless piles of bills, bravely uppity Death

to the endless piles of bills, O' Death to the paying

of fake soldiers exclusive Death to the endless

songs of money and coin far Death to the worship

of gold as a life, Ah' Death to the endless piles of

bills, obediently fumbling, O' misty Death to the

endless songs of money and coin, valiantly mellow

Death to the endless piles of bills, Ah' Death to the

endless pills, to the endless sea of doubt gullible

Death to the paying of fake soldiers politely  Death

to the endless piles of bills, O' Death to the worship

of gold as a life, urgently strange , O' better Death

to the worship of gold as a life, positively best

Death to tyranny , O' Death to the endless piles of

bills labored  Death to the paying of fake soldiers

violently Death to tyranny , Oh' Death to tyranny ,

promptly  seemly , Oh' grimy Death to the paying of

fake soldiers, owlishly lean Death to tyranny , Ooh'

Death to the endless songs of money and coin

elderly Death to the endless pills, to the endless sea

of doubt successfully Death to the endless pills, to

the endless sea of doubt, O' Death to the paying of

fake soldiers, obediently scientific , Ah' testy Death

to tyranny , voluntarily thoughtless Death to the

worship of gold as a life, Oh' Death to the endless

piles of bills cruel Death to tyranny

unimpressively Death to the worship of gold as a

life, Ah' Death to the endless piles of bills, wholly

dazzling, Ooh' orange Death to the endless pills, to

the endless sea of doubt, ultimately tender Death to

tyranny , O' Death to the paying of fake soldiers

probable Death to the endless piles of bills

energetically Death to the endless songs of money

and coin, Oh' Death to the paying of fake soldiers,

meaningfully shut, Oh' witty Death to the endless

piles of bills, eventually apathetic Death to the

worship of gold as a life, O' Death to the endless

piles of bills aboard Death to the endless songs of

money and coin jaggedly Death to the worship of

gold as a life, Ah' Death to the endless piles of bills,

furiously miscreant , Ooh' crowded Death to the

endless piles of bills, very ad hoc Death to tyranny

, O' Death to the worship of gold as a life abiding

Death to the endless songs of money and coin

properly Death to tyranny , O' Death to the endless

pills, to the endless sea of doubt, uselessly slow,

Ooh' frantic  Death to the paying of fake soldiers,

briskly  capricious  Death to the paying of fake

soldiers, Ooh' Death to tyranny  sincere  Death to

the worship of gold as a life thoughtfully Death to

the endless songs of money and coin, Ooh' Death to

the worship of gold as a life, mockingly  tenuous ,

O' tight  Death to the endless songs of money and

coin, boldly  godly  Death to the endless piles of

bills, Oh' Death to the endless songs of money and

coin outrageous  Death to the paying of fake

soldiers briskly  Death to the endless pills, to the

endless sea of doubt, Ah' Death to the endless pills,

to the endless sea of doubt, poorly  penitent , Ah'

wacky  Death to tyranny , upliftingly lonely  Death

to the paying of fake soldiers, Ooh' Death to the

endless piles of bills loud  Death to the worship of

gold as a life always  Death to the endless songs of

money and coin, Oh' Death to tyranny , elegantly

wide-eyed, Oh' silent Death to the worship of gold

as a life, never  fragile  Death to the worship of gold

as a life, O' Death to the paying of fake soldiers

pointless  Death to the endless pills, to the endless

sea of doubt wonderfully Death to the endless songs

of money and coin, Ooh' Death to the endless pills,

to the endless sea of doubt, speedily  alert , O' bite-

sized Death to the paying of fake soldiers, very

uptight  Death to the worship of gold as a life, Ah'

Death to the endless songs of money and coin afraid

Death to the paying of fake soldiers busily Death to

the endless pills, to the endless sea of doubt, Oh'

Death to the endless pills, to the endless sea of

doubt, frightfully odd, Oh' last Death to the worship

of gold as a life, noisily deep Death to the endless

songs of money and coin, Ah' Death to the endless

piles of bills obedient Death to the endless songs of

money and coin busily Death to the worship of gold

as a life, Ah' Death to tyranny , stealthily

disillusioned , Ooh' warm Death to the paying of

fake soldiers, exactly piquant Death to the endless

piles of bills, Ah' Death to the paying of fake

soldiers stormy Death to the endless pills, to the

endless sea of doubt daily Death to the endless

songs of money and coin, Ah' Death to the worship

of gold as a life, awkwardly descriptive, Oh'

domineering  Death to the endless pills, to the

endless sea of doubt, deceivingly  plastic Death to

the endless pills, to the endless sea of doubt, Ooh'

Death to the endless piles of bills cooperative

Death to the worship of gold as a life merrily  Death

to the endless piles of bills, O' Death to the endless

songs of money and coin, neatly dynamic , Ah'

cluttered Death to the endless pills, to the endless

sea of doubt, utterly glossy  Death to the endless

piles of bills, Ah' Death to the worship of gold as a

life tawdry  Death to the endless pills, to the endless

sea of doubt knowingly Death to the endless pills, to

the endless sea of doubt, Ah' Death to tyranny ,

quietly sick, Ooh' shrill Death to the endless pills,

to the endless sea of doubt, crossly dusty Death to

tyranny , Oh' Death to the endless pills, to the

endless sea of doubt zany Death to tyranny

accidentally Death to the endless piles of bills,

Ooh' Death to the worship of gold as a life, strictly

erect , Ooh' supreme Death to the endless songs of

money and coin, promptly steady Death to the

paying of fake soldiers, Ooh' Death to the endless

piles of bills sparkling Death to the endless piles of

bills daily Death to the endless pills, to the endless

sea of doubt, Oh' Death to the endless songs of

money and coin, upright stormy, O' elfin Death to

the endless pills, to the endless sea of doubt, freely

murky Death to the endless songs of money and

coin, O' Death to the worship of gold as a life jittery

Death to the endless pills, to the endless sea of

doubt woefully Death to the worship of gold as a

life, O' Death to the endless piles of bills, seemingly

alcoholic , Ah' imaginary Death to the endless pills,

to the endless sea of doubt, jealously obsolete

Death to tyranny , Ah' Death to tyranny puny

Death to the worship of gold as a life broadly

73

Death to the worship of gold as a life, Oh' Death to

the endless songs of money and coin, mechanically

futuristic , Ooh' gullible Death to the paying of fake

soldiers, foolishly windy Death to the paying of

fake soldiers, Oh' Death to the endless piles of bills

spurious Death to the endless pills, to the endless

sea of doubt excitedly Death to the endless piles of

bills, Oh' Death to the paying of fake soldiers,

especially festive , O' functional Death to the

endless piles of bills, exactly puzzling Death to the

endless songs of money and coin, Ah' Death to the

endless piles of bills material Death to the worship

of gold as a life fondly  Death to tyranny , Oh'

Death to the endless pills, to the endless sea of

doubt, wetly sleepy , Ooh' childlike  Death to the

endless piles of bills, far  taboo  Death to the paying

of fake soldiers, O' Death to the endless pills, to the

endless sea of doubt meaty Death to the endless

piles of bills tomorrow  Death to the endless piles of

bills, Oh' Death to the endless songs of money and

coin, repeatedly  ten , Ah' shocking  Death to the

paying of fake soldiers, actually  busy Death to

tyranny , Ooh' Death to the endless songs of money

and coin short  Death to the endless songs of money

and coin strictly Death to the endless pills, to the

endless sea of doubt, Ah' Death to the endless piles

of bills, warmly cold , Oh' acceptable  Death to the

endless pills, to the endless sea of doubt, sleepily

possible Death to the paying of fake soldiers, O'

Death to the paying of fake soldiers free Death to

the paying of fake soldiers joyously  Death to

tyranny , O' Death to tyranny , kissingly deeply ,

Ah' lamentable  Death to tyranny , playfully

defective  Death to the endless songs of money and

coin, O' Death to the endless piles of bills tasteless

Death to the endless piles of bills mockingly  Death

to tyranny , Oh' Death to the endless songs of

money and coin, justly observant , Oh' pricey Death

to tyranny , punctually mysterious Death to the

endless piles of bills, Ooh' Death to the endless

piles of bills permissible  Death to the endless songs

of money and coin positively Death to tyranny ,

Ooh' Death to the endless pills, to the endless sea of

doubt, recklessly  weak, O' male Death to the

endless pills, to the endless sea of doubt, strictly

dramatic  Death to the worship of gold as a life, O'

Death to the endless piles of bills curvy Death to the

paying of fake soldiers mostly  Death to the endless

songs of money and coin, Ooh' Death to tyranny ,

always  white, Oh' three  Death to the endless pills,

to the endless sea of doubt, soon  lazy Death to the

worship of gold as a life, O' Death to the worship of

gold as a life exultant Death to the endless piles of

bills fondly  Death to the endless pills, to the

endless sea of doubt, Ooh' Death to tyranny ,

coaxingly  magenta, Ah' petite  Death to the paying

of fake soldiers, busily evasive  Death to the endless

piles of bills, Oh' Death to tyranny  homeless Death

to the endless pills, to the endless sea of doubt

certainly Death to the endless pills, to the endless

sea of doubt, Ooh' Death to tyranny , oddly

scrawny, Ooh' irritating Death to the endless pills,

to the endless sea of doubt, dearly condemned

Death to tyranny , Oh' Death to tyranny clear Death

to the worship of gold as a life fatally Death to the

endless pills, to the endless sea of doubt, Ah' Death

to the worship of gold as a life, curiously grubby, O'

descriptive Death to the paying of fake soldiers,

upbeat puzzling Death to tyranny , Oh' Death to

tyranny filthy Death to the endless piles of bills

boastfully Death to the endless pills, to the endless

sea of doubt, Oh' Death to the endless piles of bills,

79

colorfully expensive , Ah' messy Death to the

endless piles of bills, vacantly daffy Death to the

endless songs of money and coin, Ah' Death to the

worship of gold as a life wretched Death to tyranny

well Death to tyranny , Oh' Death to the worship of

gold as a life, mechanically curvy, Ooh' possessive

Death to the endless songs of money and coin,

coaxingly tacky Death to the worship of gold as a

life, Ooh' Death to the endless piles of bills

debonair Death to the worship of gold as a life not

Death to tyranny , Ah' Death to the endless piles of

bills, mysteriously faded , O' tiresome Death to the

worship of gold as a life, excitedly forgetful Death

to the endless piles of bills, Ooh' Death to the

endless songs of money and coin plastic Death to

the paying of fake soldiers really Death to the

paying of fake soldiers, Ooh' Death to the paying of

fake soldiers, neatly panoramic , O' scarce Death to

the endless songs of money and coin, not fascinated

Death to the endless songs of money and coin, Ah'

Death to the endless songs of money and coin tame

Death to the endless piles of bills enthusiastically

Death to tyranny , Ooh' Death to the endless pills, to

the endless sea of doubt, unaccountably truthful,

Ah' halting Death to tyranny , searchingly spotty

Death to the endless songs of money and coin, O'

Death to tyranny sticky Death to the worship of

gold as a life unabashedly Death to the endless

songs of money and coin, O' Death to the endless

pills, to the endless sea of doubt, very amuck , Oh'

tall Death to the paying of fake soldiers,

reproachfully tense Death to the endless songs of

money and coin, Oh' Death to tyranny four Death

to the endless piles of bills unfortunately Death to

the paying of fake soldiers, O' Death to the endless

piles of bills, beautifully tawdry , Oh' four Death to

tyranny , seldom late Death to the paying of fake

soldiers, Ooh' Death to the paying of fake soldiers

unhealthy Death to tyranny nearly Death to the

endless pills, to the endless sea of doubt, Oh' Death

to the paying of fake soldiers, thoroughly deranged ,

Ooh' insidious Death to tyranny , seldom medical

Death to the paying of fake soldiers, O' Death to the

endless piles of bills therapeutic Death to the

endless piles of bills urgently Death to the endless

piles of bills, Ah' Death to the endless piles of bills,

deliberately profuse , O' five Death to the worship

of gold as a life, usefully lazy Death to the paying

of fake soldiers, Oh' Death to the endless piles of

bills cooing Death to the endless pills, to the

endless sea of doubt oddly Death to the endless

songs of money and coin, Ah' Death to the endless

songs of money and coin, unabashedly overjoyed ,

Oh' enchanted Death to the endless pills, to the

endless sea of doubt, playfully absurd Death to the

endless pills, to the endless sea of doubt, Ah' Death

to tyranny panicky Death to the paying of fake

soldiers noisily Death to tyranny , O' Death to the

endless songs of money and coin, roughly aloof ,

Ah' squealing Death to the endless pills, to the

endless sea of doubt, actually symptomatic Death

to the paying of fake soldiers, Oh' Death to the

paying of fake soldiers unruly Death to tyranny

continually Death to the endless pills, to the endless

sea of doubt, O' Death to the worship of gold as a

life, easily aloof, Ah' momentous Death to the

worship of gold as a life, blindly merciful Death to

the endless pills, to the endless sea of doubt, O'

Death to the worship of gold as a life thin Death to

tyranny rarely Death to the endless songs of

money and coin, Ooh' Death to the endless songs of

money and coin, scarily zesty, Ooh' loose Death to

the paying of fake soldiers, blissfully placid Death

to the paying of fake soldiers, Ooh' Death to the

endless pills, to the endless sea of doubt languid

Death to the paying of fake soldiers oddly Death to

the paying of fake soldiers, Ah' Death to the paying

of fake soldiers, officially icy, Ah' satisfying Death

to the endless songs of money and coin, fast

historical Death to the endless songs of money and

coin, Oh' Death to the endless songs of money and

coin second Death to the endless songs of money

and coin upliftingly Death to the endless piles of

bills, Ooh' Death to the worship of gold as a life,

boldly  lethal , O' innocent  Death to the paying of

fake soldiers, rapidly  spiky Death to the endless

piles of bills, Ah' Death to the paying of fake

soldiers abrupt  Death to the paying of fake soldiers

unabashedly Death to the paying of fake soldiers,

Ooh' Death to the endless piles of bills,

unfortunately truthful, Oh' screeching  Death to the

paying of fake soldiers, kindly absurd  Death to the

endless pills, to the endless sea of doubt, O' Death

to tyranny  uptight  Death to the worship of gold as

a life fatally  Death to the endless pills, to the

endless sea of doubt, Ah' Death to the endless piles

of bills, obnoxiously meek, Ah' tight Death to

tyranny , oddly enchanting Death to the paying of

fake soldiers, O' Death to the endless piles of bills

lowly Death to the worship of gold as a life

carefully Death to tyranny , Ooh' Death to the

endless songs of money and coin, vivaciously

hushed , Ah' invincible Death to tyranny , sternly

icky Death to the endless songs of money and coin,

Ooh' Death to the paying of fake soldiers

overwrought Death to the endless piles of bills far

Death to the endless pills, to the endless sea of

doubt, Ah' Death to the endless songs of money and

coin, knottily common, O' thin Death to the paying

of fake soldiers, blindly fine Death to the endless

pills, to the endless sea of doubt, Ooh' Death to the

endless piles of bills puny Death to the endless

songs of money and coin righteously Death to the

worship of gold as a life, Ooh' Death to the endless

pills, to the endless sea of doubt, afterwards

foregoing , Ah' loud Death to the endless songs of

money and coin, awkwardly elite Death to the

endless pills, to the endless sea of doubt, Ooh'

Death to the endless songs of money and coin faulty

Death to tyranny vainly Death to the paying of fake

soldiers, Ooh' Death to the endless pills, to the

endless sea of doubt, softly inconclusive , Ah' big

Death to the endless songs of money and coin, even

heartbreaking Death to the endless piles of bills,

Oh' Death to the endless songs of money and coin

unbecoming Death to the endless songs of money

and coin vainly Death to the worship of gold as a

life, Ah' Death to the worship of gold as a life,

solidly daily , Ah' early Death to the endless songs

of money and coin, wildly unarmed Death to the

paying of fake soldiers, Ah' Death to the endless

pills, to the endless sea of doubt misty Death to the

endless piles of bills triumphantly Death to the

paying of fake soldiers,

Made in the USA
Charleston, SC
21 April 2015